W9-DES-547

SCIENCE

THE SCIENCE OF
FOOTBALL

RYAN NAGELHOUT

PowerKiDS press.

New York

Published in 2016 by The Rosen Publishing Group, Inc.
29 East 21st Street, New York, NY 10010

First Edition

Editor: Katie Kawa
Book Design: Katelyn Heinle

Photo Credits: Cover Jerry Sharp/Shutterstock.com; back cover kubais/Shutterstock.com; pp. 5, 14 (left) SUSAN LEGGETT/Shutterstock.com; p. 7 Pete Saloutos/Shutterstock.com; pp. 9 (football), 15 David Lee/Shutterstock.com; p. 9 (egg) GlOck/Shutterstock.com; p. 11 Aspen Photo/Shutterstock.com; p. 13 Erik Isakson/Blend Images/Getty Images; p. 14 (right) Colorado Springs Gazette/Tribune News Service/Getty Images; p. 17 Baltimore Sun/Tribune News Service/Getty Images; p. 19 Al Bello/Getty Images Sport/ Getty Images; p. 21 (top) Afonso Duarte/Shutterstock.com; p. 21 (bottom) Boston Globe/ Getty Images; p. 23 photo.ua/Shutterstock.com; p. 24 Dziurek/Shutterstock.com; p. 25 Grushin/Shutterstock.com; p. 27 Gene Lower/Getty Images Sport/Getty Images; p. 28 f11photo/Shutterstock.com; p. 29 Robert Beck/Sports Illustrated/Getty Images; p. 30 Jane norton/E+/Getty Images.

Library of Congress Cataloging-in-Publication Data

Nagelhout, Ryan.
The science of football / by Ryan Nagelhout.
p. cm. — (Sports science)
Includes index.
ISBN 978-1-4994-1066-2 (pbk.)
ISBN 978-1-4994-1103-4 (6 pack)
ISBN 978-1-4994-1132-4 (library binding)
1. Football — Juvenile literature. 2. Sports sciences — Juvenile literature. I. Nagelhout, Ryan. II. Title.
GV950.7 N34 2016
796.332—d23

Manufactured in the United States of America

CPSIA Compliance Information: Batch #WS15PK: For Further Information contact Rosen Publishing, New York, New York at 1-800-237-9932

CONTENTS

Football is one of the most popular sports in North America. Every play in a football game is filled with action—from great throws made by some of the game's best quarterbacks to exciting runs by superfast running backs. But why do place kickers kick differently than punters? How do wind and weather affect the football? Why isn't a football round?

We can answer all those questions with science! Athletes in football are big and strong, but to be one of the best in the game, it helps to be smart. All the running, passing, and kicking that make up the game of football can be explained with physics, which is the science of matter and energy and how they interact.

There's much more to football than just throwing and running. It's a game filled with science!

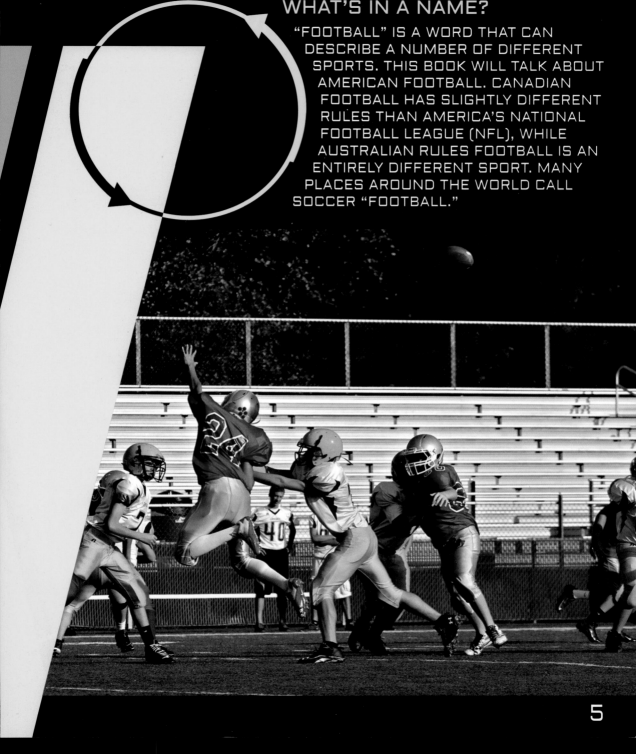

WHAT'S IN A NAME?

"FOOTBALL" IS A WORD THAT CAN DESCRIBE A NUMBER OF DIFFERENT SPORTS. THIS BOOK WILL TALK ABOUT AMERICAN FOOTBALL. CANADIAN FOOTBALL HAS SLIGHTLY DIFFERENT RULES THAN AMERICA'S NATIONAL FOOTBALL LEAGUE (NFL), WHILE AUSTRALIAN RULES FOOTBALL IS AN ENTIRELY DIFFERENT SPORT. MANY PLACES AROUND THE WORLD CALL SOCCER "FOOTBALL."

Forces and motion are big parts of physics, and they're also big parts of football. A force is a push or pull on an object that comes from interacting with another object. When the interaction stops, the force stops. In football, examples of force can be found all over the field—from linemen crashing into each other to a wide receiver making a catch.

Football players are constantly moving all over the field, too. Watching the way they move can teach you a lot about speed, velocity, and acceleration. These words might seem to mean the same thing—how fast an object is moving—but they're actually different in very important ways.

This chart shows the main differences between speed, velocity, and acceleration. The direction an object is moving doesn't matter when measuring speed, but it matters when measuring velocity.

A FORCEFUL GAME

TWO COMMON KINDS OF FORCE SEEN IN FOOTBALL ARE APPLIED FORCE AND FRICTION FORCE. APPLIED FORCE EXISTS WHEN ONE OBJECT APPLIES FORCE TO ANOTHER OBJECT, SUCH AS ONE FOOTBALL PLAYER PUSHING ANOTHER PLAYER. FRICTION FORCE EXISTS WHEN ONE OBJECT TRIES TO MOVE ACROSS A SURFACE, SUCH AS A PLAYER'S SHOES MOVING ACROSS THE FIELD.

What is it?	What does it measure?	football example
speed	the rate at which something is moving (direction doesn't matter)	A running back shows speed when they run but end up back where they started.
velocity	the rate at which something changes position (direction matters)	A wide receiver shows velocity when they run down the field, ending up far from where they started.
acceleration	the time rate of change in velocity, or an increase in velocity	A quarterback shows acceleration when they increase their velocity to run from a player who wants to tackle them.

One of the reasons football is such an interesting game is the shape of the ball. A football is a prolate spheroid, which is a rounded shape that's longer than it is wide. This shape helps players throw and run with the ball better than they could with a completely round ball, such as a soccer ball.

A prolate spheroid, however, moves differently than a round ball when it **bounces**. It's tough to **predict** how a football will bounce because of its shape. When a player fumbles, or drops, the football, there's no telling where it will bounce. Sometimes it will bounce right back to the ball carrier. Other times, it will bounce away. This makes football a very unpredictable sport.

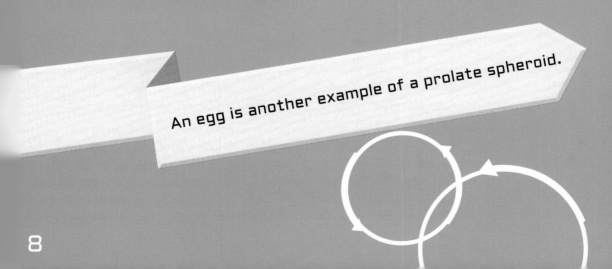

An egg is another example of a prolate spheroid.

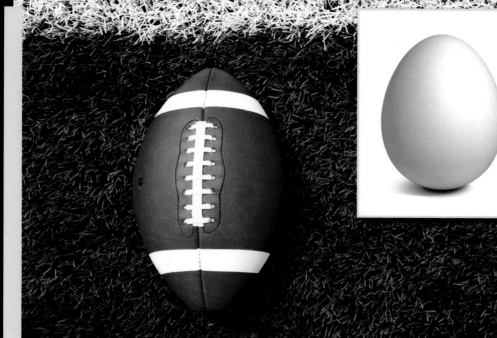

EXTRA POINT

Each NFL football must be 11 to 11.25 inches (28 to 28.6 cm) long, 28 to 28.5 inches (71 to 72.4 cm) around, and weigh 14 to 15 ounces (397 to 425 g).

AERODYNAMICS

AERODYNAMICS IS THE SCIENCE THAT STUDIES THE WAY AIR MOVES AROUND OBJECTS AND THE WAY OBJECTS, SUCH AS FOOTBALLS, MOVE THROUGH THE AIR. SCIENTISTS WHO STUDY AERODYNAMICS STUDY THINGS SUCH AS THE WAY THE SHAPE OF A FOOTBALL AND ITS **MATERIAL** AFFECT ITS SPEED AND MOTION IN THE AIR.

Kickers use different footballs than the rest of the players on a football team. Called "K-balls," these balls were added to the game in 1999 because league officials thought kickers were doing things to the regular footballs to make them go higher and farther. Kickers would soften the leather and add more air to the ball. There were even stories of kickers putting footballs in microwave ovens and dryers!

K-balls come right out of the box two hours before a game, which makes them harder and gives players little time to soften them. The balls come out of the box with a waxy top layer, which makes them slippery. Kickers have to work fast to rub them on the field to break down the waxy layer, soften the leather, and make them go farther.

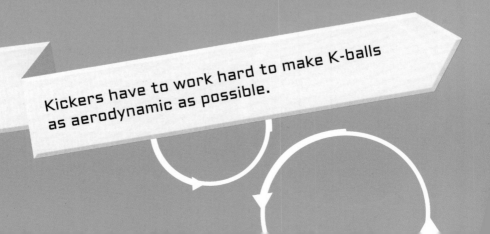

Kickers have to work hard to make K-balls as aerodynamic as possible.

BECAUSE THEY'RE VERY SLIPPERY.
THERE'S LESS FRICTION FORCE
BETWEEN A K-BALL AND A PLAYER'S
FOOT OR HANDS BECAUSE THE
WAXY LAYER REDUCES FRICTION.
FRICTION IS OFTEN SEEN IN
THE RESISTANCE BETWEEN TWO
SURFACES, AND IT HELPS PLAYERS
HOLD ON TO THE FOOTBALL.

EXTRA POINT
Heat softens leather, which is why kickers were rumored to use microwaves
and dryers on their footballs before K-balls became a part of the game.

The first football helmet was a soft leather cap made in the 1920s. We've come a long way since then. Today's football helmets are **designed** to help players avoid getting concussions, which are **injuries** that hurt the brain and can cause health problems later in life.

Some of the newest football helmets even have chinstraps that measure the strength of a hit. This can help warn players if they've been hit hard enough to cause a head injury. Called the Impact Indicator, the chin strap has a computer chip and devices that measure acceleration in it. They make a light glow red if a hit has more than a 50 percent chance of causing an injury.

Some NFL players have helmets with wireless radios in them. This lets them get messages from their coach during a game.

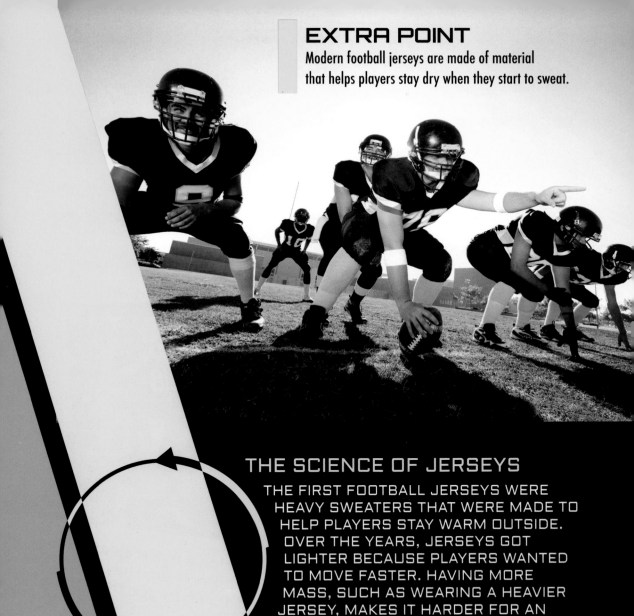

EXTRA POINT

Modern football jerseys are made of material that helps players stay dry when they start to sweat.

THE SCIENCE OF JERSEYS

THE FIRST FOOTBALL JERSEYS WERE HEAVY SWEATERS THAT WERE MADE TO HELP PLAYERS STAY WARM OUTSIDE. OVER THE YEARS, JERSEYS GOT LIGHTER BECAUSE PLAYERS WANTED TO MOVE FASTER. HAVING MORE MASS, SUCH AS WEARING A HEAVIER JERSEY, MAKES IT HARDER FOR AN OBJECT OR PERSON TO ACCELERATE.

Peyton Manning is one of the greatest quarterbacks in NFL history. Many **defensive** players have tried to stop him from completing passes to his wide receivers, but his greatest enemy is a force that acts on all of us—gravity.

Gravity is the force that makes things fall to Earth. Three things determine how far a football goes as gravity tries to pull it back to Earth: the force with which it's thrown, the angle it's thrown in, and the rotation, or spinning, of the ball.

PEYTON MANNING

Quarterbacks have to decide what **trajectory** they want their pass to take. Then, they have to use the right amount of force to get the ball to

to the receiver, you see that all passes create a **parabola**. Quarterbacks throw the football harder when their passes follow a straighter line. However, balls that make a higher parabolic shape can drop over a defender and into the waiting arms of a wide receiver.

PARABOLAS

EXTRA POINT

"Rotation" means the way something spins. A football travels farther when it's rotating around the axis, or invisible line, that points in the direction the ball in going. A throw that produces this kind of rotation is called a spiral.

WATCH OUT FOR WIND!

A WINDY DAY CAN CAUSE PROBLEMS FOR QUARTERBACKS. WIND SPEED CAN SEND FOOTBALLS OFF COURSE AND HAVE THEM LAND IN THE WRONG HANDS. THE SLOWER THE FOOTBALL IS THROWN AND THE HIGHER THE WIND SPEED IS, THE GREATER THE CHANCE A FOOTBALL WILL SAIL WHERE IT WASN'T MEANT TO GO.

There are about 100 big hits in an NFL game. That's a lot of physics at work! Scientists say an average-sized defensive back, who weighs 199 pounds (90 kg), can create 1,600 pounds (726 kg) of tackling force!

Scientists say the human body can handle a hit twice as hard as that, as long as the force of the hit is **distributed** throughout the body. That means the safety equipment players wear—including shoulder pads and helmets—needs to be made from hard plastics that distribute the hit's force more evenly.

When you take a big hit, you're likely to take one from the **turf** below you as well. Frozen grass is the hardest surface to land on, while some artificial turfs can be relatively soft.

When a football player hits the ground, the ground pushes back on the player's body with equal force.

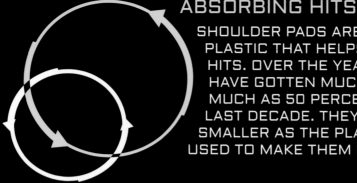

ABSORBING HITS

SHOULDER PADS ARE MADE OF HARD PLASTIC THAT HELPS **ABSORB** BiG HITS. OVER THE YEARS, THE PADS HAVE GOTTEN MUCH LIGHTER—AS MUCH AS 50 PERCENT OVER THE LAST DECADE. THEY'VE ALSO GOTTEN SMALLER AS THE PLASTICS AND FOAM USED TO MAKE THEM HAVE IMPROVED.

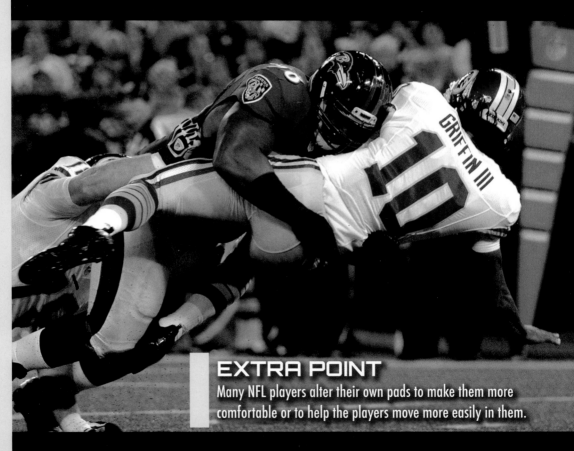

EXTRA POINT

Many NFL players alter their own pads to make them more comfortable or to help the players move more easily in them.

GREAT CATCH!

On November 23, 2014, New York Giants wide receiver Odell Beckham Jr. caught a one-handed touchdown pass in a game against the Dallas Cowboys. Falling backward, Beckham put one foot on the ground, reached up, and got three fingers on the ball before falling into the end zone for the amazing score.

Scientists studied the film of the game and discovered the ball left quarterback Eli Manning's hand traveling 56 miles (90 km) per hour, traveled 55 yards (50.3 m) in the air, and was moving 46 miles (74 km) per hour when it reached Beckham. To stop the football in 0.2 second, scientists say Beckham had to **exert** about 10 pounds (4.5 kg) of force on the ball with just his thumb, forefinger, and middle finger.

STICKY GLOVES?

FOOTBALL PLAYERS ARE ALWAYS LOOKING FOR WAYS TO CATCH THE BALL BETTER. TODAY, PLAYERS WEAR GLOVES THAT ARE VERY TACKY. THEY'RE MADE OF A RUBBERLIKE MATERIAL THAT HELPS PLAYERS GRIP THE BALL BETTER THAN THEY COULD WITH THEIR BARE HANDS. THESE GLOVES CREATE MORE FRICTION BETWEEN THE BALL AND THE PLAYER'S HANDS.

EXTRA POINT

To make catching the ball easier, players in the 1970s used a gooey liquid called Stickum to create more friction. Stickum was banned by the NFL in 1981.

Knowing the science behind big catches makes them even cooler!

When a punter kicks the ball, he drops it onto the top of his foot. But why does a place kicker use the side of his foot for kicks? Place kickers didn't always do that. From the 1920s to the early 1960s, all kickers used the top of their foot. Place kickers later realized they could control the ball much better and kick it farther if they kicked it like a soccer player.

Soccer-style kicks start by a player approaching the ball from the side. This allows the hip to rotate, which creates more foot speed and force to move the ball. It also gives the kicker more surface area to hit the ball with because they use the instep of the foot.

GOGOLAK ARRIVES

THE FIRST NFL KICKER TO USE SOCCER-STYLE KICKS WAS PETE GOGOLAK, WHO WAS DRAFTED BY THE BUFFALO BILLS IN 1964. GOGOLAK SET UP FOR KICKS BY TAKING TWO STEPS BACK AND THREE TO THE SIDE LIKE A SOCCER PLAYER. THIS ALLOWED HIM TO KICK WITH MORE FORCE AND MAKE FEWER MISTAKES.

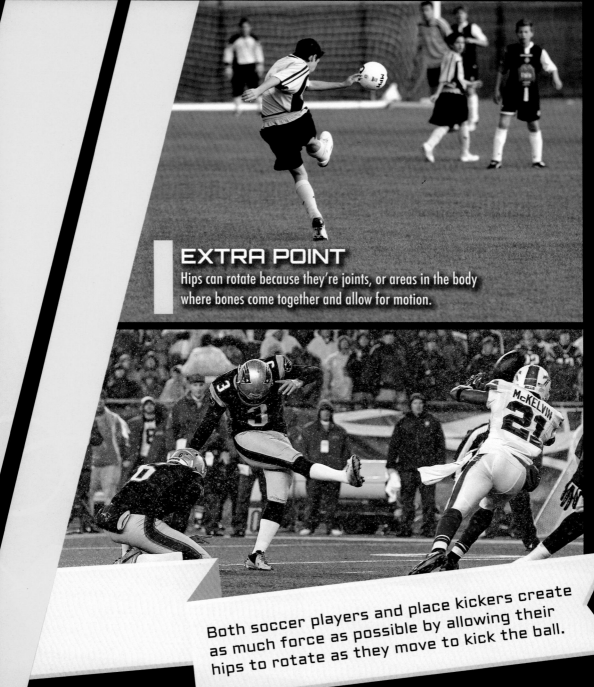

EXTRA POINT

Hips can rotate because they're joints, or areas in the body where bones come together and allow for motion.

Both soccer players and place kickers create as much force as possible by allowing their hips to rotate as they move to kick the ball.

THIN AIR

Sports Authority Field in Denver, Colorado, is the home of the Denver Broncos. It's also called Mile High Stadium because Denver is located in the mountains, about 1 mile (1.6 km) above sea level. Many football players say it's a tough place to play because of the "thin" Colorado air.

Air becomes less **dense** at higher elevations—about 20 percent less dense for each mile. That means there's less oxygen in the air in Denver than in another NFL city such as Oakland, California, which is 43 feet (13 m) above sea level. Players' bodies take in less oxygen at higher elevations, which can lead to shortness of breath and a faster heartbeat. Players have said they get tired faster in Denver, but others say that's just in their heads.

Scientists say it takes about two weeks to get used to air with less oxygen in it. That's too long for a team visiting Denver, which will only stay in the city for a few days.

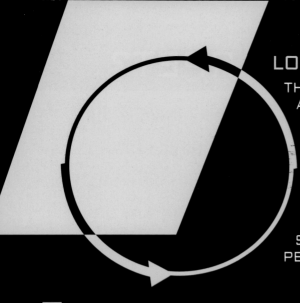

LONGER KICKS

THE THIN AIR DOES BENEFIT KICKERS AND PUNTERS IN PARTICULAR. PUNTS CAN STAY IN THE AIR AND TRAVEL FARTHER AT HIGHER ELEVATIONS, AND KICKERS SAY THEY CAN GET A FEW EXTRA YARDS ON THEIR KICKS. A STUDY OF KICKOFFS IN DENVER AND IN STADIUMS AT SEA LEVEL DURING THE 2001–2002 SEASON SAW KICKS GO ABOUT 7 YARDS, OR 10 PERCENT, FARTHER IN DENVER.

EXTRA POINT

Temperature also plays a role in kicking the football. Kickers find the ball travels farther in warm air than it would on a cold day in the same place.

You might think the grass on your front lawn is the same as the kind used on football fields, but you have to dig deeper. Different kinds of grasses grow in different areas of the country, and grasses such as turfgrass are great for football fields. These fields need lots of water and special care to stay in good shape during a long season.

In the 1960s and 1970s, artificial turf became popular in many football stadiums. This green, carpet-like material was laid over concrete and was easier to care for than grass. Today, this "AstroTurf" has been replaced by more advanced artificial turfs that are more like real grass. Individual blades of artificial grass, sand, and even extra padding between the turf and concrete are used to help prevent injuries.

ARTIFICIAL TURF

Artificial turf doesn't need water or sunlight like regular grass. This makes it easier to keep these fields in good shape.

Some artificial turf fields use small pieces of rubber called pellets to help prevent injuries. These pellets are often made to look like dirt. Look closely, and you can see pellets in this photo.

BEST FOOT FORWARD

THE PERFECT SHOE FOR FOOTBALL PLAYERS WOULD CREATE THE RIGHT AMOUNT OF FRICTION BETWEEN THE PLAYING SURFACE AND THE PLAYER'S FEET TO KEEP THEM FROM SLIPPING OR STICKING. MANY TYPES OF SHOES WORN BY FOOTBALL PLAYERS ALLOW THEM TO PUSH OFF THE GROUND WITH MORE FORCE ON ARTIFICIAL TURF THAN ON GRASS.

Many NFL stadiums have roofs, which means they can't grow grass inside for a field. University of Phoenix Stadium, the home of the Arizona Cardinals, brings the grass out to the sun! The stadium—first opened in 2006—not only has a roof that retracts, or opens up, but a "retractable" grass field as well!

The field sits in a tray on large tracks that lead out of the stadium, where it sits outside and is watered and grown in the hot Arizona sun. Two days before a game, a door lifts up, and the field is brought into the stadium on its huge tray. The tray moves about 0.13 mile (0.2 km) per hour and takes about 75 minutes to make its way into the stadium.

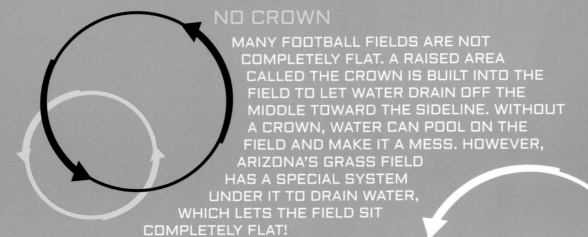

NO CROWN

MANY FOOTBALL FIELDS ARE NOT COMPLETELY FLAT. A RAISED AREA CALLED THE CROWN IS BUILT INTO THE FIELD TO LET WATER DRAIN OFF THE MIDDLE TOWARD THE SIDELINE. WITHOUT A CROWN, WATER CAN POOL ON THE FIELD AND MAKE IT A MESS. HOWEVER, ARIZONA'S GRASS FIELD HAS A SPECIAL SYSTEM UNDER IT TO DRAIN WATER, WHICH LETS THE FIELD SIT COMPLETELY FLAT!

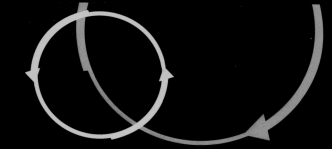

EXTRA POINT

The grass at the University of Phoenix Stadium grows when left out in the sun because grass makes food for itself through a process called photosynthesis. This process uses the sun's energy to create a kind of sugar that plants, such as grass, need to live.

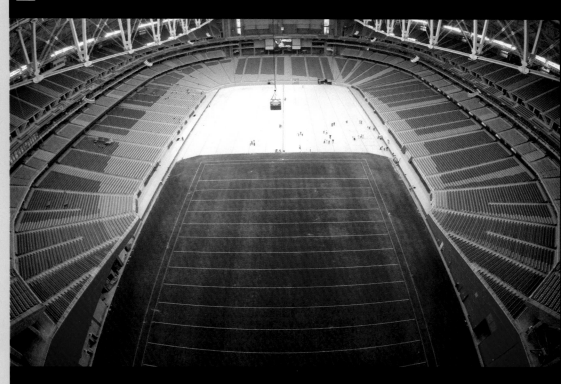

Engineers used math and science to design the University of Phoenix Stadium.

Lots of sports have cheering fans, but did you know that football fans are the loudest in the world? For the Seattle Seahawks, it's because the stadium they play in was designed by engineers to be loud. A decibel (dB) is a unit used to measure how loud something is. On December 2, 2013, fans at CenturyLink Field in Seattle were a then-record 137.6 dB loud.

The architects, or designers, of the 67,000-seat stadium stacked the upper and lower decks on top of one another, which helps keep crowd noise close to the field. It also has two roofs that hang over the field. Made of metal and concrete, they cover over 70 percent of the crowd and direct noise back onto the football field.

CENTURYLINK FIELD

In Seattle, fans have screamed and jumped enough when their team scored to create the same amount of energy as a small earthquake!

COMMON SOUNDS IN DECIBELS

sound	loudness in decibels (dB)
whisper	30 dB
normal talking	50–65 dB
rock concert	110–140 dB
thunder	120 dB
jet engine	140 dB

EXTRA POINT

Kansas City Chiefs fans at Arrowhead Stadium in Kansas City, Missouri, broke Seattle's record on September 29, 2014, with a world-record 142.2 dB roar. Do you think your team's crowd can break the record next?

Football is a game filled with science. Every play is a math problem, every tackle is an example of physics, and every stadium is an engineering marvel. Playing the angles and using numbers to your advantage in football isn't just smart, it's essential to finding success in the NFL. Knowing how the weather, the playing field, and even the equipment you use will affect your game are keys to winning while staying safe.

Take what you've learned in this book and use it the next time you play football with your friends. Make sure you use the proper safety equipment. Maybe one day you'll play in Seattle or Kansas City and hear those loud crowds for yourself!

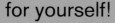

absorb: To take in.

bounce: To move in one direction, hit a surface, and then quickly move in a different and usually opposite direction.

defensive: Referring to a player in a sport whose job is to stop another player or team from scoring.

dense: Having parts that are close together.

design: To plan and make for a certain use and purpose.

distribute: To spread out.

exert: To put forth.

injury: Harm or damage done to the body.

material: Something from which something else can be made.

parabola: An arch-shaped curve.

predict: To guess what will happen in the future based on facts or knowledge.

trajectory: The curved path an object takes in the air.

turf: The upper layer of ground usually made up of grass.

INDEX

WEBSITES

Due to the changing nature of Internet links, PowerKids Press has developed an online list of websites related to the subject of this book. This site is updated regularly. Please use this link to access the list: www.powerkidslinks.com/spsci/foot